# Mariano Rivera

By Jon M. Fishman

AMAZING ATHLETES

Lerner Publications Company • Minneapolis

Lerner Publications Company
A division of Lerner Publishing Group, Inc.
241 First Avenue North
Minneapolis, MN 55401 USA

For reading levels and more information, look up this title at www.lernerbooks.com.


Library of Congress Cataloging-in-Publication Data

Fishman, Jon M.
    Mariano Rivera / by Jon M. Fishman.
       pages   cm. — (Amazing athletes)
    Includes index.
    ISBN 978–1–4677–2144–8 (lib. bdg. : alk. paper)
    ISBN 978–1–4677–2439–5 (eBook)
    1. Rivera, Mariano, 1969—Juvenile literature. 2. Baseball players—Panama—Biography—
Juvenile literature. I. Title.
GV865.R496F57 2014
796.357092—dc23 [B]                                    2013024560

Manufactured in the United States of America
1 – BP – 12/31/13

# TABLE OF CONTENTS

"You Have to Finish the Game"    4

New Position, New Job    9

First-Time Champion    13

Finishing the World Series    17

"Priceless"    22

Selected Career Highlights    29

Glossary    30

Further Reading & Websites    31

Index    32

Mariano Rivera pitches against the Boston Red Sox in 2013.

## "YOU HAVE TO FINISH THE GAME"

New York Yankees **closer** Mariano Rivera looked toward home plate. He nodded and raised his hands. Then he fired off the baseball. Boston Red Sox third baseman Will Middlebrooks swung and hit the ball to a Yankees player. He was out. But Boston's runner on third base dashed home to score. The Yankees still had a 4–2 lead in the top of the ninth inning. With two outs in the inning, Mariano needed just one more to end the game.

Mariano is the most successful closer of all time. He has more **saves** than any pitcher in baseball history. Even his **manager** is in awe of Mariano.

Mariano has been saving games for many years.

"It will be one of those thrills for me, to be able to tell my grandkids about this guy," said Yankees manager Joe Girardi.

The Yankees closer has been saving games for almost two decades. But this 2013 game was special. Mariano had missed most of the 2012 season. On May 3, 2012, he tore a **ligament** in his knee. He had surgery to repair the ligament. He was thrilled to be back on the field. "I was waiting for 11 months," Mariano said.

When Mariano enters a game at Yankee Stadium, the speakers play the song "Enter Sandman" by Metallica. The crowd roars when they hear the song.

Next up for the Red Sox was **rookie** Jackie Bradley. He couldn't keep up with the great pitcher. With two strikes against Bradley, Mariano launched a pitch across the plate.

Strike three! The game was over. Mariano shook hands and hugged his teammates.

Mariano had announced before the start of the season that 2013 would be his last year playing baseball. He was going to retire after 19 seasons. But before that, he had a job to do. "There were a lot of emotions tonight, but you have to control that," he said. "You have to finish the game."

Mariano had more than 40 saves in the 2013 season.

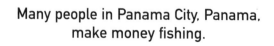

Many people in Panama City, Panama, make money fishing.

# NEW POSITION, NEW JOB

Mariano Rivera was born on November 29, 1969, in Panama City, Panama. He has an older sister and two younger brothers. Their father is also named Mariano. Their mother's name is Delia. The couple raised their children in the village of Puerto Caimito.

Soccer is the most popular sport in Panama. Mariano loved the game. He also played baseball. But he didn't take the sport seriously. "Baseball was fun," he said. "Just fun." Until the age of 12, Mariano used a piece of cardboard for a glove. Then he got a leather baseball glove as a gift from his father.

Mariano graduated from high school in 1986. He went to work with his father on a fishing boat. He didn't mind the job. But he spent most of his time daydreaming about sports. "I liked looking at all the different fish, but my father's life was not for me," Mariano said.

Mariano has brought baseball gloves as gifts for schoolchildren in Puerto Caimito. He doesn't want them to have to use cardboard as he did when he was young.

Mariano (*right*) and his dad enjoyed spending time together fishing.

In 1989, Mariano was playing **shortstop** for a local team. A **scout** from the New York Yankees named Herb Raybourn visited Panama. But Raybourn didn't think Mariano would make a good shortstop in **Major League Baseball (MLB)**.

Raybourn was back in Panama a year later. He heard about a good young pitcher named Mariano Rivera. "The Mariano Rivera I knew

Scouts such as these travel to many places to find MLB players.

was a shortstop," Raybourn said. "They told me he was a pitcher now." Raybourn set up a tryout with the young thrower.

Mariano still remembers the tryout. "It feels like it was yesterday," he said in 2009. He also said he wasn't nervous. "I had nothing to lose."

Raybourn liked what he saw the second time. On February 17, 1990, Mariano signed a **contract** with the Yankees. He received $3,500 in the deal.

Mariano was happy to sign with the Yankees.

The 2013 Gulf Coast League champions pose for a photo. Mariano played in this league when he first came to the United States.

# FIRST-TIME CHAMPION

Mariano left Panama for the United States in 1990. It wasn't easy for him to leave home. His mother also had a tough time with the move. "I was worried," Delia said. "At that time, we didn't have phones in this town, so he wrote us and told us how he was. I think it was hard on both of us."

The young hurler wasn't ready to join the Yankees. First, he had to prove himself in the **minor leagues**. From 1990 to 1994, Mariano played for minor-league teams in Florida, North Carolina, New York, and Ohio.

Mariano plays catch at spring training in 1996.

The New York Yankees finally called up Mariano near the beginning of the 1995 season. The Yankees made him a relief pitcher. This meant Mariano wouldn't be the pitcher who started a game. Instead, he would come into a game in the later innings.

Mariano pitched well as a rookie. But in 1996, he became one of the best pitchers in the game. He served as the **setup pitcher** to closer John Wetteland. Mariano pitched mostly in the eighth inning. In just over 107 innings, he struck out 130 batters. His **earned run average (ERA)** was an incredible 2.08.

Mariano pitches against the Minnesota Twins.

The Yankees made it to the **playoffs** and then to the World Series. They faced the Atlanta Braves. The Braves won the first two games in New York.

Mariano's most common nickname is Mo. He's also known as the Panama Express.

The Yankees celebrate their 1996 World Series victory.

But the Yankees won the next four games in a row. Mariano and his teammates were world champions! They took a victory lap around Yankee Stadium as the fans screamed.

Years later, a reporter asked Mariano to name his favorite moment at Yankee Stadium. "That's an easy one," the closer said. "The end of the World Series in '96. Why? Because it was the first one."

Mariano smiles after getting knocked down by the ball in a game against the Texas Rangers.

# FINISHING THE WORLD SERIES

John Wetteland left the Yankees after the 1996 season. This meant New York needed a new closer. They chose Mariano. The team was confident he could do the job. After all, the role wasn't very different from being the setup pitcher.

Mariano fires the ball in the ninth inning.

"Mo used to be our closer in the eighth inning," said former Yankees pitching coach Mel Stottlemyre. "Now he's our closer in the ninth."

In 1997, Mariano racked up 43 saves as the Yankees' new closer. His ERA was a sparkling 1.88. Mariano saved 36 games in 1998. Even better, the team won the World Series for the second time in three years. They took down the San Diego Padres in four games.

The Yankees knew they had someone special in Mariano. They signed him to a new contract in 1999. He would be paid $4.2 million. Mariano was rich!

Mariano and the Yankees won the World Series once again in 1999. In 2000, New York made it to the World Series for the third straight year.

Mariano married his wife Clara in 1991. The couple has three sons: Mariano, Jafet, and Jaziel.

Mariano pitches during Game 1 of the 1999 World Series.

They battled the New York Mets. People called it the Subway Series because of the underground trains that connect different parts of New York City.

The Yankees jumped ahead, three games to one. The fifth game was tied 2–2 until the ninth inning. Then the Yankees scored twice to take the lead. In the bottom of the ninth, Mariano came in to finish the World Series.

Mariano got two outs. But he would have to face Mike Piazza with another Met on base.

Yankees player Jorge Posada (*right*) slides home during the 2000 World Series.

Piazza was the Mets' best hitter. Yankees shortstop Derek Jeter jogged to the pitching mound. He

Derek Jeter (*left*) and Mariano have fun on the field.

slapped Mariano with his glove to encourage him.

Mariano threw a pitch. Piazza swung and launched the ball deep into the outfield. But Yankees player Bernie Williams ran under the ball. He caught it. The Yankees were World Series champions for the third year in a row!

Mariano watches the throw to second base.

## "PRICELESS"

By 2001, most baseball fans agreed that
Mariano was the best closer in the game.
Some people even called him the best ever.

And he was on one of the best teams of all time. The Yankees went to the World Series for the fourth year in a row.

New York seemed unstoppable. They won three games. But so did the Arizona Diamondbacks. It would all come down to the seventh game. Mariano entered in the bottom of the ninth inning. His team had the lead, 2–1. He had previously saved 24 playoff games in 25 chances.

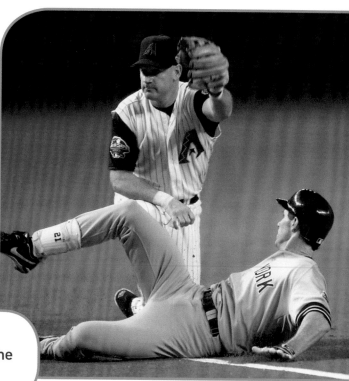

Yankees player Paul O'Neill (*below*) is tagged out during the 2001 World Series.

But this time, it didn't work out for Mariano and New York. Arizona scored two runs to win the game and the World Series.

Mariano was disappointed. But great closers must put losses behind them and focus on the next game. That's what Mariano did. He saved at least 28 games each season between 2001 and 2011. He helped his team win another World Series in 2009.

Mariano pitches in the 2010 MLB playoffs.

Mariano got a special save on September 19, 2011. He closed out a game against the Minnesota Twins for the 602nd save of his career. This made Mariano the top closer in baseball history.

Mariano celebrated after the game in the **dugout**. Then his teammates pushed him back out to the pitcher's mound.

Mariano tips his cap to the crowd after notching his 602nd save.

The Yankees are the most successful team in MLB history. They've won the World Series 27 times. No other team has won the World Series more than 11 times.

The fans had stayed to cheer for their amazing pitcher. "For the first time in my career, I'm on the mound alone," Mariano said later. "There's no one behind me, no one in front of me. I can't describe that feeling because it was priceless."

Mariano announces that he will retire after the 2013 season.

Mariano laughs with fans before a 2013
game against the Boston Red Sox.

Mariano decided the 2013 season would be his last. Fans applaud him at every stadium he visits as one of the all-time greats. Many teams have given Mariano gifts to honor his career. But Mariano also takes time to visit with people who work behind-the-scenes at baseball games.

Mariano waves to his fans.

"I appreciate what you guys do," he told a group of ticket sellers in Cleveland in 2013. Baseball fans have appreciated what Mariano does for almost two decades.

# Selected Career Highlights

**2013**  Named to All-Star Game

**2012**  Missed most of season with knee injury

**2011**  Named to All-Star Game
Set all-time saves record

**2010**  Named to All-Star Game

**2009**  Named to All-Star Game
Helped New York win the World Series

**2008**  Named to All-Star Game

**2007**  Finished tied for 8th in MLB in saves (30)

**2006**  Named to All-Star Game

**2005**  Named to All-Star Game

**2004**  Named to All-Star Game
Led MLB in saves (53)

**2003**  Finished 3rd in MLB in saves (40)

**2002**  Named to All-Star Game

**2001**  Named to All-Star Game
Led MLB in saves (50)

**2000**  Named to All-Star Game
Helped New York win the World Series

**1999**  Named to All-Star Game
Led MLB in saves (45)
Helped New York win the World Series

**1998**  Helped New York win the
World Series

**1997**  Named to All-Star Game

**1996**  Helped New York win the
World Series

# Glossary

**closer:** a pitcher who usually comes in at the end of a game when the pitcher's team has the lead

**contract:** a deal signed by a player and a team that states the amount of money the player is paid and the number of years he plays

**dugout:** shelters where the players sit on the sides of baseball fields

**earned run average (ERA):** a statistic that measures the number of runs a pitcher allows per nine innings. For example, if a pitcher pitches nine innings and gives up three runs, the pitcher's ERA would be 3.00.

**ligament:** a short, flexible band that connects two bones

**Major League Baseball (MLB):** the top North American professional baseball league

**manager:** the head coach of a baseball team

**minor leagues:** leagues below the major-league level in baseball. Players work to get better in the minor leagues before joining their major-league team.

**playoffs:** a series of games after the regular season to determine a champion

**rookie:** a first-year player

**saves:** a statistic that measures how often a relief pitcher helps his team win close games

**scout:** someone who judges the skills of athletes

**setup pitcher:** a pitcher who usually comes into a game in the eighth inning

**shortstop:** a baseball player who takes the position in the field between second and third base

# Further Reading & Websites

Doeden, Matt. *The World Series: Baseball's Biggest Stage*. Minneapolis: Millbrook Press, 2014.

Donovan, Sandy. *Derek Jeter*. Minneapolis: Lerner Publications Company, 2011.

*The Official Site of Major League Baseball*
http://www.mlb.com
Major League Baseball's official website provides fans with the latest scores and game schedules, as well as information on players, teams, and baseball history.

*The Official Site of the New York Yankees*
http://newyork.yankees.mlb.com/index.jsp?c_id=nyy
The New York Yankees official site includes the team schedule and game results, late-breaking news, biographies of Mariano Rivera and other players and coaches, and much more.

*Sports Illustrated Kids*
http://www.sikids.com
The *Sports Illustrated Kids* website covers all sports, including baseball.

# Index

Atlanta Braves, 15

Boston Red Sox, 4–7

Girardi, Joe, 6

Jeter, Derek, 21

minor leagues, 14

New York Mets, 20
New York Yankees, 4–7, 14–21, 23–24

Panama, 9, 13
Piazza, Mike, 20

Raybourn, Herb, 11
Rivera, Delia, 9, 13
Rivera, Mariano: childhood of, 9–11; and baseball history, 25–28; and minor leagues, 13–14; and the World Series, 17–21, 23–24
Rivera, Mariano (father), 9–10

Stottlemyre, Mel, 18

Wetteland, John, 15
Williams, Bernie, 21
World Series, 15–16, 18–21, 23–24

# Photo Acknowledgments

Photographs used with the permission of: © Jim McIsaac/Getty Images, p. 4; © Jared Wickerham/Getty Images, p. 5; © Jim McIsaac/Getty Images, pp. 7, 24, 29; © Adeliepenguin/Dreamstime.com, p. 8; © Ronald C. Modra/Sports Imagery/Getty Images, p. 10; AP Photo/Matt Slocum, p. 11; © Ron Antonelli/NY Daily News Archive via Getty Images, p. 12; Cliff Welch/Icon SMI 357/Newscom, p. 13; © Mitchell Layton/Hulton Archive/Getty Images, p. 14; © Al Bello/Allsport/Hulton Archive/Getty Images, p. 15; © Henny Ray Abrams/AFP/Getty Images, p. 16; Laura Cavanaugh UPI Photo Service/Newscom, p. 17; © Don Emmert/AFP/Getty Images, p. 18; © Linda Cataffo/NY Daily News Archive Getty Images, p. 19; © Jeff Haynes/AFP/Getty Images, p. 20; AP Photo/Mark J. Terrill, p. 21; © Otto Greule Jr./Getty Images, p. 22; © Matt York/AFP/Getty Images, p. 23; © Rob Tringali/MLB Photos via Getty Images, p. 25; AP Photo/Kyodo, p. 26; © Barry Chin/The Boston Globe via Getty Images, p. 27; © Patrick McDermott/Getty Images, p. 28.

Front cover: © Thomas Levinson/MLB Photos via Getty Images.

Main body text set in Caecilia LT Std 55 Roman 16/28.
Typeface provided by Adobe Systems.